Lariats and Lassos

Lariats and Lassos

Bernard S. Mason's
How to Spin a Rope

WESTPHALIA PRESS
An imprint of Policy Studies Organization

Lariats and Lassos:
Bernard S. Mason's *How to Spin a Rope*

Westphalia Press
An imprint of Policy Studies Organization
dgutierrezs@ipsonet.org

For information:
Westphalia Press
1527 New Hampshire Ave., N.W.
Washington, D.C. 20036

ISBN-13: 978-1935907077
ISBN-10: 1935907077

Updated material and comments on this edition can be found at the Policy Studies Organization website: http://www.ipsonet.org

BERNARD S. MASON

———

BERNARD S. Mason wrote books on woodcraft, drums, tomtoms, rattles, boomerangs, teepees, wigwams, but more than that he was in ways the spiritual father of American camping. Professor Mason got his Ph.D. from Ohio State University and then taught there, writing voluminously as the philosopher of American camping enthusiasts. He founded Camp Kooch-I-Ching in Minnesota, which continues to this day, and the Camping and Education Foundation perpetuates this legacy.

HOW TO SPIN A ROPE

Lariat Throwing, Rope Spinning
and Trick Cowboy Knots

by

BERNARD S. MASON

Published by
BERNARD S. MASON
Columbus
1 9 2 8

Printed in the United States of America

PREFACE

This little book attempts nothing more than to present roping as play. It has made a serious effort at every turn to bring the joy and romance of rope spinning and lariat throwing within the range and capacity of the average boy and girl, and to point out the play possibilities involved in the various uses of the lariat.

Acknowledgment is made to The Country Gentleman and The American Boy for the privilege of using several photographs which have already appeared in those magazines in connection with articles by the writer. The writer is also deeply indebted to Albert W. Field for much of the photography involved in producing the illustrations.

BERNARD S. MASON.

Ohio State University
Columbus
June, 1928.

CONTENTS

CHAPTER I

How to Throw a Lariat

Where is there an American boy or girl whose heart does not beat a little quicker at the thought of the American West in its wildest and most romantic days, with its bucking bronchos, its long horned steers, and its flying lariats? Or at the sight of the picturesque sombreroed cowboy riding with the ease and skill which are distinctly his? The American West is all our own — strictly American in its every aspect — no other nation can boast of anything resembling it in picturesqueness or ruggedly romantic qualities.

And just because it is all our own, just because it is strictly American and withal so ruggedly virile and masculine — we, all of us, long to do the things which pertain to the West: especially does practically every American boy long to rope, to be able to handle the lariat as Fred Stone, Will Rogers, and our other western heroes do. Yet how few are able to do it! How few American boys are able to even throw a lariat, let alone to spin one or jump through its loop. Surrounding the art of lassoing are the finest traditions of our western pioneer days — it is a sport for a man, sufficiently difficult to challenge the athletic ability of any one. Yet not so difficult but that any boy or girl can become reasonably proficient at it provided he or she has the right kind of a rope and is willing to work.

Roping is not limited to men alone. The girls who have mastered the art, particularly of rope spinning, are

9

almost as numerous as the men, and the appeal it makes to them is no less profound. Roping as a sport has much to recommend it to women.

I have never yet seen a man or woman who caught the lariat fever and was able to shake it off. In fact it grows worse as the years go by. Once we get started at it, so fascinated do we become that we are loath to quit until every trick in the business is mastered. And that is the task of a life time.

And all the time we are roping we are getting a splendid workout, for the ropes are stubborn and they make you sweat. A half hour of fast rope spinning is workout enough for any man.

But exercise and muscle are not the only values in roping. Fred Stone tells me of the time when he was practicing with his ropes on some tricks for his shows, out behind his Long Island home, when suddenly he heard frantic screams from the swimming pool on the back part of his estate. His rope still in hand, he rushed over to find a man struggling and sinking about twenty feet out from the shore. A swing or two of his rope, and the noose was slapped down over the clutching arms. The rope saved the fellow's life much easier and more quickly than any swimmer in America could do it.

Again Fred tells of the time when his pack horse lost his footing in a swift mountain stream and was rolling over and over like a ball toward the water fall some twenty feet below. A quick cast of the noose, and the beast was snubbed to a sapling, his life and outfit saved.

A lariat and the ability to handle it is a most valuable part of the equipment and education of outdoor men and women. The rope should go on every trip into the woods. Sometime you may be able to save a drowning companion, or some day you may be able to rope a mountain lion in the Grand Canyon or a polar bear beyond the Arctic Circle—such things are not at all impossible. But best of all, whenever you pick up the lariat, you are sure to rope a lot of fun and plenty of splendid exercise.

In this little book we are not at all concerned with training ourselves to become cowboys and cowgirls, nor in describing just how the cowboy worked in the old days on the ranch, but we are interested in roping as a sport—roping for fun and for exercise—hoping to acquaint more boys and girls with the joy and fascination of this art of the old-time West.

Roping is romance; it is health, joy, vigor; it is picturesqueness, color, high adventure. It is American, and should be part of the outdoor education of every American boy and girl.

How to Make a Lariat

I sat for an hour in my room the other afternoon watching a boy trying to rope an old packing box out in the alley behind our house. The poor fellow did not know the first principles of handling a lariat and his efforts to snare the box with the old clothes line he was using were pathetic. Finally I took pity on him and went out with my ropes and showed him the inside on the trick. A day or two later I saw him out in the same alley, this time with a brand new rope, which he was dropping on the box quite regularly.

The trouble with this boy in the beginning was large-

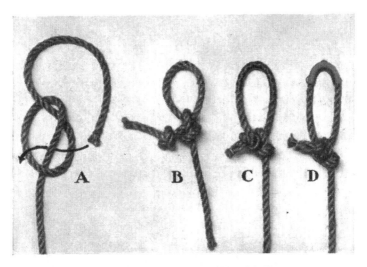

1. HONDAS USED ON CATCH ROPES.
A & B—METHOD OF TYING THE LARIAT LOOP.
C—WIRE ADDED FOR PROTECTION AGAINST WEAR AND TO
INCREASE WEIGHT.
D—A METAL HALF HONDA USED FOR WEIGHT.

ly in his rope: the best roper in America could not have done much with the old clothes line he was using. Just any rope one happens to pick up will not make a lariat. Trying to use the clothes line has discouraged many a boy and girl ambitious to become a roper. For throwing, secure 35 feet of new manilla rope, ⅜ inch thick, at any hardware store. There are other types of rope used in roping (See Chapter IV), but there are none of them suitable for a beginner to start practice with. The ⅜ inch manilla rope is the ideal practice rope. Buy one. Splendid ready-made manilla lariats are on the market, but be sure you specify ⅜ inch.

Tie a lariat loop at one end, forming the eye or "honda". To do this, a simple overhand knot is tied as in Picture 1, Figures A and B, and the end passed through as indicated by the arrow. Study the photographs carefully and you will get the method. The eye thus formed should be from 3 to 4 inches long. Tie an overhand knot on the end to prevent it from pulling out Jam the whole knot as hard as possible. Now pass the other end of the rope through the honda and you will have a lariat, or lass-rope, or riata, or soga, or just plain rope as those who use it frequently are most prone to call it. "Lasso" is seldom used as a name for a rope; it is a verb and refers to the act of throwing a rope. "Lariat" comes from the Spanish "La riata".

No, you do not need a brass or metal honda on the throwing rope. That is the mistake so many begin-ners make. Such a heavy honda would render the rope practically useless for our purpose. After one has become a good roper and wants to weight his rope on the end for certain uses, he can easily do so by wind-ing a little wire around the honda. Brass hondas have their use but not on throwing ropes of this type. Many a horse has had his eye knocked out with these heavy metal hondas, and many a boy has injured his play-mate with them.

A still better honda can be made by doubling the end back and splicing it there with an eye splice. This is much less common than the lariat loop, however, due probably to the fact that few cowboys know how to splice.

A little wire wound round the end of the honda as in Figure C, Picture 1 prevents wear, as well as adding a little weight, which is often desirable.

Bill, who was a little shaver in camp and just learning to rope, foolishly sank the noose of his lariat over
the head of one of the camp's peppy young riding horses
who wasn't used to ropes, cowboys and such things. No
sooner had the noose settled than the colt's heels were
up in the air and he was off across the pasture field with
the unfortunate and much dazed Bill dragging on the
ground behind him. What happened was that the
knot which Bill had tied on the "home" end of his rope
to prevent it from unraveling had caught somewhere in
his shirt or belt or top part of his trousers (he doesn't
know yet just where, nor how) and before he realized
what was happening he was on the ground and bound-
ing his way over the bumps. Being the little runt
that he was, his weight furnished little resistance to
the frenzied horse, who tore most of the way around
the circle of the "ranch" before Bill was able to dis-
entangle himself from the rope. The mistake Bill made
was in putting the knot on the end of the rope. Knots
have a habit of doing such things. What he sould
have done was to lash the end with a piece of twine.
Had he been on horseback the knot might have caught
somewhere in his saddle or trappings and both he and
his horse given an expected upset.

The Wind-Up Throw

We are now ready to rope. Holding on to the
honda, throw the rope out on the ground and shake
the kinks and twists out of it. Now shake out a noose
in the right hand as in Picture 2. The noose should
be roughly four or five feet long, the exact length as
it hangs making very little difference, and the honda
should hang about half way down or a little more.

2. THE NOOSE ON THE CATCH ROPE READY TO BE THROWN.

Be sure the honda is on the outside — the side away from you. That is important. Now with the noose all arranged, coil up the lariat with the left hand, taking the coils in the right hand. Each coil should be about 15 or 18 inches long. When the coiling is com-

3. COILING—GIVE THE ROPE A HALF TURN WITH YOUR FINGERS EACH TIME YOU LAY A COIL IN.

pleted transfer the coils to the left hand, as in Picture 4, taking the end between the thumb and finger. This coiling should be carefully done so that the rope will run out smoothly from the hand when it is thrown.

4. HOLD THE COILS IN THE LEFT HAND.

To be able to coil a lariat neatly and quickly is an accomplishment in itself, and there is a little trick to it which can be easily picked up. As you hold the noose in your right hand as in Picture 2 and bring the coils around with your left hand, give the rope a half turn toward you with your fingers each time as you lay it in your hand, as indicated in Picture 3. This makes the coils lay flat in your hand and prevents the kinking which is so annoying.

17

5. READY TO THROW.

For the position you are in just before throwing, study Picture 5 carefully. Standing in this position, swing the noose up and around overhead as in Picture 6. This is your wind-up. You do it for much the same reason that a pitcher winds up in baseball — it

18

6. THE WIND-UP SWING.

gives you steadiness and helps your aim. Furthermore, it opens the noose for the throw. This swinging is done with a right to left motion — that is, as the noose passes in front of you it is moving from your right to left. As you swing it in the air you can let out more rope and thus enlarge the noose until it feels in your your hand to be about the right size for the

7. STEP FORWARD AND THROW STRAIGHT AT IT.

throw. Just how big the noose should be depends upon what you are throwing at — one has to learn to judge this from experience. Two or three swings should be sufficient.

Let us suppose that we are roping a post in the back yard: having wound up, step straight toward the post and throw. Keep your eye on the top of the post and throw straight at it. Do not throw in the general direction of the post and trust to luck that the noose will hit it: **Put it there.** Just as in baseball some players fail to bat consistently because they take their eyes from the ball a fraction of a second before the bat connects, or would have connected, so in lariat throwing you must keep your eye on the target constantly, from the time you start the wind-up until the noose hits or misses. You may do nothing more than wrap the rope around yourself the first time, but never mind that. Stay with it.

At the start it is best to stand not more than ten feet away from the post. Gradually you can work back to thirty feet, which is a good distance to test one's skill. It is the usual maximum distance for roping, although the Texas cowboys sometimes succeed in making catches at forty or even fifty feet.

If these instructions are being followed, all you will have to do is to keep working. It will come to you before you know it. There is only one secret in roping, and that is work. To become a good roper you must practice, practice, practice. For my part, I never admit to myself that I can do anything of this sort until I can do it fifty times in succession on several successive days. Keep score on yourself as you practice: How many times out of twenty-five can you rope the post? Then how many out of fifty? Do not stop today until you have beaten yesterday's record.

You may have trouble at times in getting the loop to open for you as you swing it in the air. This is due to the fact that the rope is twisted. When such is the case there is no use trying to throw, nor is there any use putting your foot on the noose and trying to stretch the kinks out of it as amateurs are wont to do. Slide the honda down to the end, and, taking it in your hand, unwind and shake the twists out. Then re-coil and the noose will stay open. It takes time and is annoying, but there is no other solution.

The Straight Throw or Toss

Another method of lariat throwing is the toss or straight throw, which is a cast without a wind-up, and is really much more useful and convenient than the wind-up method; in fact, in the actual roping of animals it is indispensable. Experienced ropers seldom use the wind-up except on horseback. To walk into a corral of horses swinging a noose around one's head preparatory to throwing would be the height of folly; it would work the horses up into a frenzy and make it exceedingly difficult to single out the one desired. Instead the rope must be thrown from the ground without any preliminary swinging. The wind-up is the usual method on horseback, but is seldom used on the ground.

Arrange the rope as for the wind-up throw, and stand as in Picture 8. Note that the palm of the hand holding the noose is up and that the noose is well to the rear. From this position step toward the post with

8. ARRANGEMENT FOR THE TOSS OR STRAIGHT THROW.

the left foot and throw the noose over and down on it without any preliminary swinging. At the start it is better to stand about six feet from the target and toss the noose over on it until the wrist develops the right motion. With a little practice this method be-comes much easier and more fascinating than the wind-up.

The Left to Right Throw

Roping an animal around the neck with either the wind-up throw or the toss is a simple task, provided he is facing you or headed toward your right. If he is headed toward the left, however, the task is much more difficult and requires the left to right throw.

Arrange the rope as before, holding the noose in your right hand, but wind up by swinging it from left to right — that is, as the noose passes in front of your body, it is moving from left to right. Cast so that the noose approaches the target from the left.

Roping Moving Targets

With the development of skill in handling the rope, posts and stationary targets soon become uninteresting and we want the challenge of a moving object. Dogs, calves, pigs, chickens — in fact everything in the neighborhood that could run — were pressed into service by the writer. It is in working on these dodging targets that we really develop skill in manipulating a rope and find the greatest joy in lariat throwing. The fascination is greatly increased, however, if we have learned the art of roping by the feet.

Roping by the Feet

The trick and fancy roping of the rodeos calls for the stunt of roping horses by the feet.

Have you ever watched the circus cowboys do it? If you have, you sort of wished you were a cowboy with a flock of horses, and could do the thing yourself. You can, and you do not even need a horse to practice

9. WAITING FOR HIM.
10. AFTER HIS FEET.

on; you can rope the feet of a running boy and get just as much of a thrill out of it as if he were a bronc.

Tell the boy who is going to run for you to come fast and pick his feet up high. Let us hope that he is good natured and does not mind being tripped up now and then, for he can help you a great deal if he will. He will probably be "rope shy" at first — that is, just as you throw for his feet he will unconsciously and un intentionally slow up or shy away from you, thus caus ing you to miss. To prevent this, place a stick on the ground about ten feet in front of you and have him run over it. But caution him about slowing up and trying to hurdle or jump over the rope.

Shake out a big loop on the ground, at least six or eight feet across for beginners, and arrange as in Pic ture 9. **Note particularly that the back of the roper's hand which is holding the noose is toward the runner.**

Now let him come and yell to him to come fast. Just as he passes throw the rope over and down at his feet, as in Picture 10. **Note that the back of the roper's hand is still toward the runner.** He has not just swung his arm around parallel to the ground; rather, he has brought it over and down, turning his wrist as he threw so that the back of his hand and consequently the same side of the loop is toward the runner. That is the difference between throwing to rope him by the head and by the feet. In throwing for his head you throw straight at it, while in catching his feet you turn your wrist and get him with the back side of the loop. Try it a time or two: it is not as hard as it sounds.

If you timed it right the loop will be there waiting for him as he passes and he will step right into it.

26

Really, he ropes himself. All you do is to toss the noose over and have it waiting for him. It will take a little practice to time it just right. You will probably throw too soon at the start — it is better to wait a little too long, if anything.

What if the boy is coming from the opposite direction? You make precisely the same movements as before. The palm of the hand holding the noose will, of course, be toward the runner as you rope him now, for he is coming from the other direction, but your wrist will be in exactly the same position as before.

Roping Several Runners

A favorite stunt of the trick-roping cowboys of the rodoes is to catch several horses running side by side in a rope. This is by no means a difficult stunt, and any one who can rope one boy should have no difficulty in roping several (Pictures 11 and 12). Have the boys lock arms to keep them close together, and tell them to sprint as fast as possible. Shake out a real big loop, and throw it just as you would if only one boy were running. Start by roping two boys, then add one at a time until you can manage six or seven.

Roping Horses

Roping a horse by the feet is in no wise different from roping a running boy; exactly the same movements which caught the boy will catch the horse. Make the loop sufficiently big, and step right up and rope him.

Of course, you will have to have a rider for the horse who will put him past you within roping distance while you practice. If your horse will canter past without

11-12. All FIVE OF THEM BY THE FEET.

28

stopping short or shying when the rope is thrown you are indeed fortunate. We watch the fancy trick ropers and marvel at their skill, but we forget that some of the credit is due the horse and the man who is riding him. These roping horses are specially trained and the rider has worked with the roper so long that he knows just what to expect. There are some horses

which could not be ridden for roping in a hundred years, but most horses soon get used to the rope. Some will not shy in the least, even at the start. The best trick roper in the world could not catch a horse consistently if he stopped or shied past him, so do not be too severe with yourself if you miss now and then with a green horse. Put him past at a good fast canter, about eight or ten feet in front of you.

All Four Legs

As soon as the rope hits the horse's feet, pull up quickly and you will have him trapped by the front legs. If you throw a big loop and hesitate just a second before pulling up you should have him by all four legs, which is a pretty and spectacular piece of roping. Having pulled the rope tight, drop it and let it drag on the ground. The rider should immediately pull up the horse and stop him, remove the rope and ride back for the next catch.

Roping Horse and Rider

Toss a big noose over the horse's head so that it falls behind the rider, circling both the rider and the horse's neck.

Horse's Tail

A clever stunt with which the trick ropers often conclude their exhibitions is to rope the horse by the tail. Use a small noose, and just as the horse canters by, flip it up against his hind legs, snaring him by the tail. Of course, you will have to stand very close to the side of the horse as he passes.

Fancy Trick Roping

Fancy roping includes both lariat throwing and rope spinning. When the rope spinning stunts in Chapter 2 have been mastered, particularly the Ocean Wave (Page 57) and the Skip (Page 58), it is possible to spin the rope for a few seconds while the horse is coming up, and then to rope him with the spinning noose. These tricks require years of practice and are beyond the scope of the average amateur.

The Maguey Rope

The best quality ⅜ manilla rope recommended for the above tricks is the ideal practice rope for beginners, but those who develop a real interest in roping will probably want a Maguey rope (pronounced ma´gay), which is a Mexican handmade rope of agave fibre. It is unexcelled for lariat throwing and trick roping. Chapter IV contains the details regarding this rope, which is very inexpensive and can be obtained from any cowboy outfitters.

CHAPTER II

How to Spin a Rope

When Vincenti Orespo (or maybe it was Oropeso), a Mexican cowpuncher, came over to this country a few years ago and signed up with Buffalo Bill's Wild West Show, rope spinning was a thing unheard of. (I am not so sure about how this Mexican spelled his name— Fred Stone tells me it was Oropeso, while Will Rogers has it as Orespo; for our part, we shall call him Vincenti). Anyway, ever since the first herd of cattle grazed its way across the western prairies, lariats were an indispensable item in the cowboy's equipment, but it was not until this Vincenti put himself on exhibition for Buffalo Bill that it occurred to any one that a rope could be spun.

It was not so long ago that Vincenti came—rope spinning is really a very modern wrinkle in the use of the lariat. He was not a finished rope spinner, this Mexican; not by any means. But he was a bangup straight roper, and did a lariat throwing act which knocked the pins out from under most of our American cattle chasers. And in the course of his act he introduced a simple rope spinning trick or two which he had invented back home and incidentally showed to the world for the first time that a lariat could be spun.

Our American cowboys were not slow in picking up this new kink, and soon had stolen the Mexican's thunder, for they developed the stunt of rope spinning far beyond his wildest dreams, evolving in time the present day intricate art with its almost limitless variations, as we witness it on the stage today when we see Will Rogers, Fred Stone, or the Wild West shows. The American ropers were the first to jump through a rope.

Lariat throwing is one thing; rope spinning is something else. Lariat throwing is useful in catching horses and cattle on the ranches, and was indispensable in the early days. But rope spinning has no practical value, aside from the fact that it is splendid exercise and a wonderfully fascinating sport.

"I'd sure like to go on a ranch out West and see the cowboys spin a rope," said a boy friend of mine the other day as he was perspiring over a stubborn lariat which refused to spin for him.

When this boy's dream is realized, if it ever is, and he makes his trip to the western ranches, he will doubtless be distinctly disappointed, for search as he will he may not be able to find a single rope-spinning ranch hand (unless he goes to some of the dude ranches employing show cowboys), but he will find plenty of fine straight ropers who can rope and hog-tie a steer in less time than it takes us to tell about it. If he should single out the ranch boss and ask him why this is so—why none of his cow hands can spin a rope, he would soon find out in no unmistakable terms. Should the ranch boss hire a man who can spin a rope he would have all the cowboys on the place spinning ropes—in fact, little else but rope spinning would happen if the men had their way, and the ranch work would be sorely neglected. So the ranch boss is uninterested when a fancy rope spinner applies for a job, and as soon as a man demonstrates his ability along this line too often he usually moves along soon to another ranch.

But as sport and recreation, rope spinnig is more appealing than straight roping could ever be. There are so many different tricks and endless variations which add color and variety, and present constantly new challenges to one's skill and athletic ability. Then, too, it gives one a work-out.

In learning to spin a rope, a smooth floor will be a big asset. Do not attempt it in the drawing room, however, especially if you are particular about the polish and fixtures, and do not practice in clothes which you expect to use for any other purpose. A rope has the habit of picking up all the dirt on the floor. Girls should wear knickers — a skirt will be constantly interfering with the rope.

Making the Spinning Rope

In rope spinning, the rope is all important. One cannot pick up just any rope and hope to succeed. Most men have tried at some time in their lives to spin a rope but without success. The reason, no doubt, lies partly in the fact that their rope was not adapted for that purpose. A manilla throwing rope is useless for spinning. Have you ever seen Will Rogers, Fred Stone, Hank Durnell, or some other artist in a lariat spinning exhibition? If you have you will recall that he picked up a separate rope for almost every series of tricks he attempted. Without the just-right rope for the particular trick we are learning our efforts are very likely to be futile. One finds this out more and more as he progresses. The writer has worked for weeks, while learning to spin a rope, on a certain trick

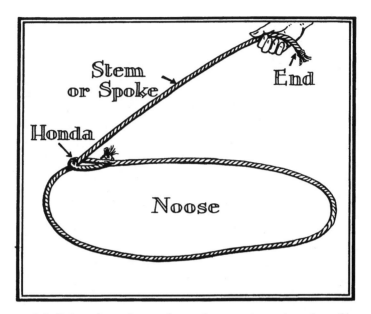

and failed, only to learn through experimenting that the rope was not right for that particular trick. With the proper rope success would have come in a few days.

A specially prepared braided cotton rope is needed for successful spinning, this can be obtained from your dealer made up in the proper length. The best size for most of the tricks is 3/8 inch, commonly designated as No. 12, although the No. 10 size is suitable for small boys. Both sizes, made up in the proper lengths and weights to meet the demands of these tricks can be obtained from your dealer or a manufacturer of spinning ropes.

For the beginner at rope spinning, 20 feet of rope is about the right length. The roper in the frontispiece is using 20 feet. A small boy may find 17 or 18 feet a better length. Secure 20 feet and after a trick or two

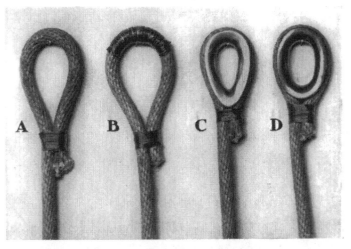

15. HONDAS USED IN SPINNING ROPES
(a) WIRED HONDA. (b) ADDED WIRE FOR WEIGHT.
(c) LIGHT ALUMINUM HONDA. (d) HEAVY BRASS HONDA.

have been learned, if the rope seems too long, cut it down. It is not wise for an amateur to try to use a long rope by holding it short. Cut it off.

Bend one end back and wire it there with copper wire, forming an eye or honda, about 3 inches long, as in Figure A, Picture 15. Pass the other end through the honda and the rope is ready to use. Some ropers prefer a light weight aluminum honda (Figure C), but they are not at all essential.

The Body Spin

Let us start by learning the body spin or "wedding ring", illustrated in the frontispiece, which is not only one of the most spectacular spins in itself, but is the basis of many other tricks which we shall want to learn. Twenty feet of 3/8 inch cotton cord is required.

16. READY TO START THE BODY SPIN.

Hold the rope as in Picture 16. Study the picture carefully. Note that the extreme end of the rope is in the right hand, held between the thumb and finger,

17. LAY IT OVER THE HEAD WITH THE RIGHT HAND, KEEPING THE LEFT HAND LOW.

18. DROP IT DOWN TO THE LEVEL OF THE WAIST.

40

19. GIVE IT A CIRCULAR SPIN AROUND YOU.

the other fingers holding the noose, and that the left hand merely holds the noose open. Also note that the honda is nearly down to the ground on the right side. The stem held in the righ hand goes straight through the honda and is not doubled back as so many begin-ners think.

Pick the noose up with the right hand and lay it over your head, as in Picture 17, **keeping the left hand low.** Do not use the left hand to lift the noose up — that is the fatal mistake every beginner makes: **The left hand must remain on the level of your waist in the entire process.** Much strength is not necessary—just lay the noose over your head with the right hand so that it circles the body.

Having laid it over your head, drop the right hand quickly down until the rope is on the level of the waist as in Pictures 18 and 19, then give the noose a hard spin around you from right to left, using both hands to give it momentum. As you do this let go with your left hand and release the noose with the right hand, hold-ing on to the end only. Raise your right hand over-head and just keep it going.

Too much muscle is sure to mean defeat. It is spun largely with a wrist motion, not an arm motion. Your arm should be perpendicular overhead, perhaps with a slight bend at the elbow, and little motion is made with it — the wrist mainly keeps it going. A wide violent arm swing breaks the spin — it is the fault hardest for most beginners to overcome, and perhaps much of your failure at the start may be traceable to it.

At first you will succeed only in wrapping yourself up in the rope, but don't be discouraged at that. Keep at it. There is no easy road to roping. Every one who spins the rope has paid the price and you will have to do the same. The price in roping is hours of practice. So keep at it and it will come, perhaps much sooner than you expect. And when it does, practice harder than ever. Don't admit you have learned it until you

20. THE BODY SPIN OR "WEDDING RING".

can start the spin fifty times in succession without breaking down.

Body Spin with Either Hand

When you have the rope spinning around you nice-ly, reach up and take the stem in your left hand and keep the spin going, thus giving your right hand a rest. Practice changing hands until you can work as easily and smoothly with one hand as with the other.

Hand Shaking

This clever little trick which the boys in some parts call Hand Shaking should be learned next, and is a very simple yet quite spectacular variation of the body spin. Starting from the body spin, it consists of dropping the spinning loop to within a few inches of the ground and keeping it spinning there by passing the stem around the body from one hand to the other. Picture 21 shows it in action.

Get the body spin going nicely and just as the stem is passing the right shoulder, drop the spinning noose to the ground by lowering the right hand to the level of the belt. Grab the stem quickly in the left hand and carry it around behind you; reach around with the right hand, take it and bring it around in front, where the left hand takes it again, and so on. It takes some fast grabbing with the hands. Try doing it on a smooth floor at first.

The Flat Spin

Having mastered the body spin and gotten the "feel" of the spinning rope, we are now in position to take up the flat spin, which is in reality easier than the other

21. HAND SHAKING—PASS THE STEM FROM ONE HAND TO THE OTHER.

45

22. ARRANGEMENT FOR THE FLAT SPIN.
23. THE FLAT SPIN.

46

and will doubtless be learned in a few minutes. It consists of spinning the rope in front of the body as in Picture 23.

The same rope used for the body spin is ideal for the flat spin (See page 37). Arrange the rope as in Picture 22. Note that the noose is quite small, the end of the rope extending over to the left hand.

Keeping the left hand practically in place, flop the noose over with the right hand so that it is parallel with the ground and in the same motion give it a spin from right to left. Let go of the loop with the left hand, holding on to the end only. This initial spin which you give it must be a circular motion — your hand must cut a circle in the air of about the same size and shape which the spinning loop is to have. It is as if you took hold of a prostrate bicycle wheel and gave it a spin. But after you once get it going it is all a wrist motion.

When you can do the flat spin nicely with the right hand, pass the spinning rope to the left hand and continue until you can do it equally well with either hand.

In the flat spin the rope can, of course, be easily spun in either direction. As described above, it is spun counter-clock wise. With a little practice you can make it spin in the opposite or clock wise direction.

Jumping In

Now that we have learned the flat spin it is possible to step into the spinning noose if we are clever enough, as illustrated in Picture 25. But you must step at just the right moment or the stem will hit you as it spins around. The time to step is just as the stem starts toward you — by the time you have jumped it will be past you and out of the way.

24. READY TO STEP.
25. STEPPING IN.

In Picture 24 the stem is in just the right position to jump — it is away from the spinner and just starting toward him. Picture 25 shows where the stem is by the time he has stepped.

The trick is not to jump up in the air and pull the spinning noose toward you — that would break the spin. Instead, you must step into it. The spinning rope remains in the same place—you merely step over into it.

Once inside, raise the right hand overhead and do the body spin.

A rope 17 or 18 feet long may be a little handier in learning this trick and the one that follows.

Jumping Out

Having started with the flat spin and jumped into it, the next trick is to step out. This is done by dropping the spinning noose to the ground and stepping back out of it.

In doing the body spin, just as the stem posses your right shoulder, drop the noose to the ground by lowering your right hand to near the belt, and immediately step backwards and over the spinning rope, picking up the spin in front of you again.

After you have stepped out of the noose, the rope will be spinning in exactly the same place as before — the noose is not moved forward, rather you yourself step backward and out of it Now you can step right back into it again.

In learning these tricks of jumping out and in it is best to practice at first on a smooth floor, but eventually you will be able to do it without letting the noose touch the floor.

The Juggle

The juggle is one of the most picturesque and fascinating of the rope spinning tricks, both to the spinner
himself and to the spectators. The juggle is the body
spin except that the spinning noose is dropped to the
floor, then raised up overhead as far as it will go, pulled
down to the floor again, then up again, and so on, in
rapid succession. It is often a little difficult for beginners to learn, largely because they do not know the
details of the trick, but by following these instructions
it should be easy.

Picture 26 shows the juggle on the way up.

Using the same 20 foot rope with the wired honda
with which the preceding tricks were done, get the
body spin going nicely, and then start lowering and
raising it, very slightly at first. This lowering is done
entirely by the shoulder. Keeping your forearm
straight overhead as in the body spin, lower the arm
a little at the shoulder just as the stem passes the right
shoulder, then raise it as high as you can reach. Keep
this up until you can raise and lower your arm at the
shoulder slightly without breaking the spinning noose.

When you have accomplished this much we can
try the real juggle. Just as the stem is passing your
right shoulder drop the noose to the floor as in Hand
Shaking (Page 44), but instead of changing hands
give the rope a spin there and raise it right up again,
bringing the stem up behind the left shoulder. In
raising your hand up reach as high overhead as possible, then drop the noose to the floor again. The rope
must spin around rou three times on each trip up or
down—once near the floor, once while passing the

50

26. THE JUGGLE, GOING UP.

51

waist, and once over head. We must keep time with the spinning noose in raising it; we cannot rush it—it must have plenty of time to do the three spins at a steady uniform rate of speed. It is well to count while learning—one for the lower spin, two for the one around the waist, three for the high one and four for the middle one going down. Take it easy and do not be discouraged—it will come to you soon. When the noose is at its lowest point, be sure to bive it a spin there before you start to raise it.

When you can raise the noose up and down, you will want to get a new rope better adapted to the trick and with which you can do a more spectacular juggle. Secure 25 feet of No. 12 spinning rope equip-ped with a metal honda, obtainable through your dealer or a manufacturer of spinning ropes. The rope is fitted around the honda and wired as in (Figure D, Picture 15). Now try the juggle and see the change—the metal honda gives it weight and you can raise and lower the loop in rapid succession and throw it as high overhead as the stem will permit. This same rope is what is needed for some of the tricks we are going to learn later (particularly the Skip, Page 58). Do not attempt to convert the 20 foot light-honda rope into a juggle rope by adding a heavy honda; you will want that rope for the many other tricks for which it is adapted.

Overhead and Down

Here is a trick which to the spectator seems extremely difficult and which sounds most difficult to the reader, but as a matter of fact it is not especially so. It consists of tossing the spinning nooe up over the head, and down in front of the body, keeping it spinning there.

Start from the flat spin in front of you and get the noose spinning rapidly. Step into it as you did in Picture 25 and just as you do so raise your arm up quickly, tossing the noose away up over your head as in Picture 27. Look up at it as the roper is doing in the picture. Note where the stem is and give it one spin up there, then throw it down on the floor in front of you. Instantly pick it up and keep the spin going. After a few times you will be able to catch the loop in the air in front of you and not let it hit the floor.

If you give it a good spin as you step into it, and keep your eye on it over your head, giving it a spin up there, you will have no difficulty in mastering this one and you will have learned a headline trick.

27. UP AND OVER.

While doing the body spin you can, of course, toss the rope up over your head as in the juggle and down in front of you.

Juggling in Head-First

Get the flat spin going rapidly in front of you, raise the noose up over the level of your head, step under it and pull it down into the body spin. When you are doing the flat spin in front of you, your hand holding the stem is above the noose, of course. As you raise the noose you must pull your hand with the stem quickly around and under it. This is a more difficult trick and requires practice.

Merry-Go-Round

In learning the merry-go-round we are starting on one of the most delightful series of tricks in roping, and one which no one interested in the art should fail to learn. It is by no means a difficult trick to master for it has as its basis nothing more difficult than the flat spin. The trick consists of carrying the flat spinning noose all the way around the body. Picture 28, showing the two handed merry-go-round, gives an idea of how this trick looks in action.

For this trick the 20 foot rope with the wired honda is needed, although a 16 or 18 foot one is a better length. Get the flat spin going nicely as described on page 44, then carry the spinning noose past your left side, around behind and to the front again, by raising your arm up over your head and reaching behind. At first you will have trouble in making it spin behind you, but this is doubtless due to the fact that you are rushing it too much behind for fear that it will not get around you.

Do not worry about the noose not getting past your back — it will float around of its own accord if you

28. MERRY-GO-ROUND, TWO HANDED. THE STEM HAS JUST BEEN
PASSED FROM THE LEFT HAND TO THE RIGHT.

simply carry your hand back over your shoulders. The main concern is to keep the rope spinning—not to carry it around the body.

Starting the spin in front of you with the right hand, carry it well to the rear of your left side, keeping your eye on it, and there give it one good spin — don't jerk it to get it past your back — just spin it, and then gently carry your hand past your shoulders, turning your head around to the right side. The rope will float past your back and be still spinning when it reaches the right side. Here pick up the spin again and carry it around in front. This jerking the stem to get it past the back is the disastrous mistake most beginners make. At the start, it is better to carry the noose around the body in five spins, but later four may work out to be more satisfactorily.

When you have the merry-go-round mastered, you can work up a series of tricks around the flat spin, featuring the body spin, hand shaking, juggling, jumping into and out of, throwing the loop over head and down, and the merry-go-round. Work from one into the other without stopping the spin. Never let the noose stop spinning while working before spectators if you can help it. The following two tricks work into this series also.

Two Handed Merry-Go-Round

This is a variation of the merry-go-round described above. Get the rope spinning in front of you with the right hand, take it in the left hand and carry it around behind you, there take it in the right hand and carry it around in front where the left hand takes it again, and so on. In Picture 28, the rope has just passed from the left hand to the right hand. If you have mastered the straight merry-go-round, this one can be learned in fifteen minutes.

Ocean Wave

The ocean wave is one of the most famous of the spinning tricks and is on exactly the same principle as the merry-go-round. The difference lies in the fact that the noose, instead of spinning parallel to the ground, is more or less perpendicular to it. A rope with a slightly heavier honda often makes this trick easier; the honda can be made heavier by winding a little wire around the rope inside of the eye.

In preparing to start the ocean wave, swing the noose around over your head a time or two as if you were preparing to throw a lariat, then release the noose and start spinning. The motion started by swinging the rope will carry the spinning noose around you. The merry-go-round can also be started in this way.

Lay Down

While spinning the rope around you with the body spin (Page 37), sit down on the ground very slowly and carefully, and gently straighten your legs out on the ground under the spinning loop. Then drop down to a reclining position on your left elbow, as in Picture 29. With a little practice you can lay flat on your back. A 15 or 16 foot rope is best.

Retiring

This trick, popular among the circus cowboys, consists of taking one's coat off while doing the body spin, rolling it up ,and laying down on the ground, using the coat as a pillow. The trick is finished by getting up and putting the coat on again.

29. TAKING IT EASY.

While doing the body spin with the right hand, work the left arm out of the coat, then take the rope in the left hand and work the right arm out.

The Famous Skip

This is the headline roping trick of them all — the famous skip with which the circus cowboys never fail to thrill the crowds. Since it is the most spectacular of the tricks, it is the one which all ropers are most anxious to accomplish.

It takes a pretty good kind of individual to do this stunt, one who is somewhat of an athlete and is willing to work a little and stick. It will require practice — to some many, many long hours of practice — but that makes it all the more worth doing. I know many boys and some girls who have mastered it.

It might have been a Mexican cowpuncher who introduced the idea that a rope could be spun, but it was the American cowboys who first jumped through a spinning noose. In fact, as we noted above, most of the difficult and intricate tricks of rope spinning, as our experts do it today, were originated by our American ropers.

Although it is not based on any of the other spins, it is best not to attempt the skip until some of the easier tricks, such as the body spin and flat spin, have been mastered. Having become thoroughly familiar with these and gotten the "feel" of the spinning rope in its various positions, you will be ready to accept the real challenge of roping which is offered by the skip.

The skip lariat consists of about 22 feet of No. 12 spinning rope of the best quality, equipped with a brass honda (Figure D, Picture 15). The rope used in the body spins and similar tricks will not do. Do not attempt to transform this old rope into a skip rope by adding a heavy honda — save it for the tricks for which it is adapted and secure a new rope for skipping. A brass honda can be obtained through spinning rope manufacturers. Metal eyes are obtainable for a few cents at hardware stores, but the chances are they will be too light. It will be better to send for a brass honda made for use on spinning ropes.

A rope of just the right size and weight is all-important for this trick—without it one cannot hope to succeed. Splendid ready-made skip ropes designed especially for this trick are on the market.

30. ARRANGEMENT FOR THE SKIP.

Hold the rope as in Picture 30. Note that the noose is rather small, the end extending over into the left hand. Later you can start it larger, but this is the size for now. Note also just where the honda is. Now with a hard spin from right to left give the rope

31. READY TO JUMP. 32. FAMOUS SKIP.

61

a whirl and let the noose go, keeping it spinning with a wrist motion. Let out rope rapidly until it is all out as in Picture 31. The weight of the heavy honda will keep it going in the vertical position must easier than one might think if the rope is balanced properly. But you must give it its initial spin with a distinct circular motion, just as if you took hold of an inverted bicycle wheel and gave it a spin.

Do not attempt to jump through until you can spin it perfectly and easily in this position. When you have accomplished this, turn your left side toward the spin- ning rope as in Picture 31, and you are in position to jump. Now it is a case of perfect timing—unless you jump at the just-right moment the stem will be in the way, as can be easily seen. As the stem is going **down** on its way around—**just as it nears the bottom of its downward motion**—is the time to jump and pull the noose toward you. If you timed it right—jumped at the just-right moment—it will have passed around you without touching and still be spinning on your right side as in Pictures 32 and 33. As the stem is going down, it, of course, is in the way of your jump; but by the time you have jumped it will have passed down and be going up in front of you, and hence out of the way.

The trick is not done by jumping toward the noose but rather by jumping straight up in the air and pull- ing the spinning noose toward you. Be sure to get your feet well up off the ground and out of the way.

With a little practice you will be able to tell when the time to jump arrives by the feel of the rope. There is no way of acquiring the ability to jump at the right time except by practice. Use your head as well as your

arm—study each failure and attempt to find where the mistake lies.

When you have mastered this jump you have half of the trick learned; the second part consists of jumping back, bringing the rope back to its original position again. The rope is now on your right side, of course. Just as the stem is going **down** on its way around, jump and pull the rope toward you, bringing it back to the left side as before.

This is about all that it is possible to tell in writing about how this splendid trick is done. The many little knacks about it can only come through practice. No, you'll not get it the first time you try, nor the second, perhaps not the hundredth, but keep at it. For

34. THE SKIP.

everything that's worthwhile you must pay the price. The price in roping is hours and hours of practice. If you pay it, you'll get it.

Rope spinning, to do it completely and well, is a life-time proposition. There are so many different spins. Every roper, no matter how long he has been at it, is constantly learning some new wrinkle about it. So don't expect to learn it over night.

Running Skip

It is possible to run while skipping, taking a few steps between each jump. This requires much practice.

Skip and Turn

This variation is even more spectacular than the straight skip. It is performed exactly like the straight skip except that as you jump, you turn the body in the air so that the same side is always toward the noose.

Stand as in the straight skip with the left side toward the spinning noose (Page 58 and Picture 31). Jump and pull the nose toward you as before, but as you do so, turn the body in the air so that when the jump is over the left side is still toward the rope. Jump back and turn the body again, always keeping the left side toward the spinning noose. Be sure you have the straight skip thoroughly mastered before attempting this.

Butterfly

The butterfly requires the rope with the light honda used in the body spin. The trick consists of spinning a small noose in a vertical position two spins on the left side, throwing it over to the right side and doing two spins there, and so forth. It can also be done by spinning one spin on each side. These intricate tricks with the small noose are more or less difficult and should not be attempted by begginers until most of the other tricks are mastered.

Rolls

The rolls are exceedingly difficult spins to master and require constant practice. They consist of spinning a small noose either horizontally or vertically, and rolling it over the shoulders when the head is bent forward, across the chest when the head is bent back, and over either arm. Many rope spinners do not consider the rolls important or spectacular enough to be worth the effort required in perfecting them.

Hurdling

This interesting trick is well worth the effort required in mastering it. It does not call for any difficult rope spinning, but does require considerable general athletic ability. Use the skip rope with the brass honda.

Start the flap spin in front of the body near the ground and step into it as in Picture 25. Immediately stoop down so that the stem and spinning noose are as near the ground as possible, and jump the stem each time it comes around. A smooth floor will be a great help in learning this trick. It is possible to make progress as you hurdle, thus moving across the floor.

The Big Loop

One of the facinating tricks of roping is the spinning of the big loop, using anywhere from 50 to 100 feet of rope in the body spin. One can easily spin 60 to 70 feet standing on the ground, but for the longer lengths it is usually necessary to stand on an elevation such as a horse's back or a stump.

These big loops require a small size of rope—cotton sash cord No. 10—and an extra heavy honda. Use a brass honda as on the skip rope (Figure D, Picture 15), but double the rope back around it so that it overlaps at least 5 inches; wire this end to the main rope with copper wire, covering it solidly with wire from the honda to the end. The honda and wire together supply the weight necessary to keep the big loop going.

67

Start a small noose spinning as in the regular body spin, and let out rope rapidly until the entire length is in action. It takes a lot of strength.

Sitting Skip

This exceedingly difficult trick which some professionals do consists of jumping in and out of the spinning noose while sitting on the floor. It does not require so much in the way of rope spinning ability, but is exceedingly difficult as a physical feat. Few men do it.

Two Ropes

When one gets well along in roping and has mastered most of the standard tricks, he usually likes to try his skill at spinning two ropes, one in each hand. Use two short loops for this, about 12 to 15 feet long. Start out by doing a flap spin with each rope, and then one vertical and the other flat. Later you may be able to spin one rope in one direction and the other in the opposite direction.

One of the best of the two rope tricks is to do the body spin with the left hand and the hurdle with the right.

As a rule, however, if a person spins one rope and does it well he is doing plenty.

CHAPTER III

Trick Cowboy Knots

Did you ever see the cowboy in the vaudeville show throw a fancy knot into the end of a rope with a twist of the wrist, using only one hand, so quickly that the eye could not detect the method? It is like a trick of magic—now a straight rope, the next instant a fancy knot. It is a clever trick of the Wild West boys, yet one which any one can learn with a little practice. It is all in knowing how.

In tying these trick knots it is best to use a spin-ning rope with a brass honda, although they can be done with an ordinary honda formed by wiring the end back. The weight of the brass honda is a great help, particularly to a beginner.

The Pretzel

The most fascinating and spectacular of the trick knots is the pretzel. Hold the lariat as in Picture 36, allowing it to hang down about three or three and a half feet. Note that the palm of the hand is up. Now turn your wrist over quickly, throwing the rope across the back of your arm forming a loop as in Picture 37, Practice this motion until you can do it quick-ly and easily before trying the second half. Then, in the same motion with which you turn your wrist over, jerk the honda up in the air and catch it in the loop as shown in picture 37.

Study the pictures—they tell the story better than words can do.

36. START FROM THIS.
37. METHOD OF TYING.
38. PRETZEL
39. FIGURE OF EIGHT.

70

Shake it off your arm and let it fall and you have the famous pretzel (Picture 38), or perhaps you will have the figure-of-eight. Just which one you will get will be a matter of chance at the start, for they are tied in exactly the same way, but if you shake it off your wrist gently and do not jerk it as it falls, the pretzel should be the result.

Practice this knot until you can do it like a flash. To do it slowly makes the stunt look cheap. And remember, you have not learned it at all unless you can do it fifty times in succession without a miss. You will be surprised how this little trick will impress the spectators.

Figure-of-Eight

The figure-of-eight (Picture 39) is tied by precisely the same movements as the pretzel described above. Pictures 36 and 37 illustrate these. The factor determining which knot will result is the way the knot is dropped after shaking the rope off your arm. Jerk it as it falls and you should have the figure-of-eight. Shake it off gently and the pretzel should result. The figure-of-eight tends to result if a brass honda is being used, since the weight of the honda gives it a jerk as it falls, while a pretzel is the usual result when a light honda is employed. However, with a little practice either knot can be tied at will with the same rope.

Practice for speed in tying these knots. The hand is always quicker than the eye, and if you are fast with the rope the trick becomes very impressive.

The Overhead

Easier and simpler than the pretzel or figure-of-eight is the overhand (Picture 41). Hold the rope, palm up,

40-41. METHOD OF TYING THE OVERHAND.
42-43. METHOD OF TYING THE SLIP.

72

as in Picture 36, allowing it to hang down about three feet. Turn your wrist over quickly, throwing the rope across the back of your arm forming a loop as in Picture 40. So far it is exactly like the pretzel. Now reach down with this loop and catch the honda as indicated by the arrow. Do not try to jerk the honda up through the loop: reach down under it and drop it through.

Practice until you can do it very quickly. Otherwise it loses its attractiveness as a stunt.

Slip Knot

The ordinary slip knot (Picture 43) can be tied as a lariat trick also, and any one who can tie the overhand described above will find it exceedingly simple. Do not try it until you have mastered the overhand.

Just as you are about to catch the honda in doing the overhand, shove the standing part of the lariat held in the left hand under the honda and in back of it. (Picture 42). Then complete by catching the honda as in the overhand. Compare Picture 42 with the overhand illustration in Picture 40, noting the position of the standing part of the lariat in the two. With a little practice you will be able to shove the rope over with the left hand so quickly that the spectators will not detect the use of the left hand in the trick.

Flying Overhand

This trick consists of tying an overhand knot in the end of a 30 foot lariat by holding on to one end and throwing a half hitch in such a manner as to catch the loose end, thus forming the knot. Lay the rope out in front of you, jerk the end toward you, and at the same time throw an overhand half hitch down the rope, through which the end passes forming the knot. Use plenty of slack in throwing the half hitch. This knot requires a great deal of practice and is often discouraging. It has little value, being neither useful nor especially spectacular.

CHAPTER IV

Types of Lariats and Their Care

Just what tribe in the history of mankind was the first to use the lariat, and exactly what materials were used in its construction are questions which we cannot answer with authority. But the development of the lariat seems to be closely associated with the history of the horse—the handling of animals necessitated the use of rope of some type. And since it was evidently around the horse that the lariat was evolved, the chances are that the materials used were either horse-hair or rawhide, both of which are obtainable from the animals themselves. Many think the most primitive rope was horsehair.

Horsehair and Rawhide Lariats

Hair lariats were extremely common in the early days of the west and in Mexico, and are still made occasion-ally by the Mexicans and certain tribes of Indians. Friends of mine tell me that among the French peasants of some sections horsehair lariats are still in common use today. They are a rare article among the roping cowboys in this country. however, being more diffi-cult to produce, more expensive, and less efficient than modern hemp rope. Then, too, hair ropes are often a little light in weight for good roping, and are inclined to wear up rough with use, not to speak of their ten-dency toward kinking. While they served their pur-pose in the early days, they have not been able to com-pete with modern rope for strength or efficiency, and are seldom seen outside of the wild west shows and the curio shops where they help to make the picture of the old time West. They can still be purchased through the manufacturers of spinning ropes.

The standard rope of the pioneer days of the West was the rawhide lariat, made of buffalo or horse hide. Although rare, there is an occasional ranch hand today who finds these old time sogas more to his liking than any of the modern inventions. Rawhide lariats are frequently extremely heavy and cumbersome, as compared with hemp rope, and often have a weak spot in one of the strands which eventually breaks, rendering the entire rope useless.

In making these leather riatas, the hides were stripped up into long throngs, which were either twisted together as in modern hemp rope, or plaited with a four or eight plait. Much pounding and rolling was necessary to get them smooth, round, and even, and much greasing to soften and water-proof them. The Mexicans make them yet, and they can be purchased through the manufacturers of spinning ropes and lariats.

Hemp Lariats

Modern hemp rope so far excells the hair and raw-side lariats that it has almost completely replaced them. Today the catch ropes of the cowboys are made of best quality long fibre hemp.

In Chapter I a 35 foot manilla rope, ⅜ inch, was recommended as the best catch rope for beginners to practice with. In actual roping a 7/16 inch rope is used, ranging in length from 35 to 45 feet. For beginners to attempt to use one of these heavy long ropes

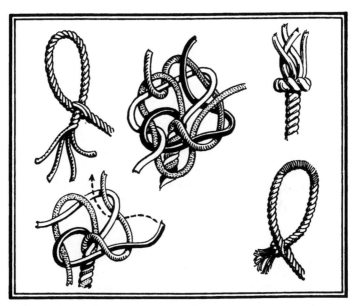

44. HONDA FOR THE MAGUEY ROPE.

would be a mistake, although with the development of skill one can gradually work up to them. In some sections of the southwest ropes as long as 50 feet are found, but they are not by any means universal.

The Maguey Lariat

The finest rope obtainable for trick roping and all around use by one interested in roping as a sport is the Mexican maguey rope, obtainable from any cowboy outfitters at a very small cost. These are handmade ropes of agave fibre, four strand, and about ⅜ inch thick. They are hard and smooth in finish, and sufficiently stiff to hold a beautiful noose. Maguey ropes

77

are thoroughly to be recommended to every one interested in learning to rope. After the beginner's stage
with the 3/8 inch manilla rope is over, the maguey will
supply endless satisfaction.

A special type of honda is used on the maguey rope
because of its stiffness and the fact that it is four-
strand. This is made by separating the strands with a
spike, two on each side, and passing the end through
the opening thus formed. The strands of this end are
then unraveled and a tucked wall knot tied with them,
thus preventing the end from pulling out. Figure 44
illustrates the method, and the construction of the wall
knot. Wire the honda as illustrated to add weight.

Braided Cotton Lariats

With the invention of rope spinning in recent years,
the braided cotton sash cord lariat came into prom-
inence. It is the only spinning rope, but, of course, is
useless for any of the other purposes to which lariats
are put.

"Breaking In" New Rope

Any kind of new rope needs to be "broken in" or
conditioned before it will work efficiently. Otherwise
it will be full of kinds and twists. This is usually done
by tying it behind a wagon or on a saddle and letting
it drag in the dirt for half a day. Stretching it between
two posts with weights fastened to it for a day or two
is a method sometimes used also. Spinning ropes do
not need this strenuous treatment—they usually break
in quickly with use, but all hemp and maguey riatas
should be conditioned in this way.

Dampness

Rain and dampness render manilla rope practically useless for catch purposes—it becomes limp, lifeless, after it had dried out. Catch ropes used in actual roping are waterproofed when new by greasing with vaseline, or treating with paraffin waterproofing. The average beginner practicing with a new manilla rope will not want to go to this trouble, and will not need to for his rope will stand up for a long period if he takes care of it and does not let it lie out in the dampness when not in use.

Wet spinning ropes are impossible—they should never be allowed to get damp.

The maguey rope when wet or even when slightly damp becomes exceedingly stiff and wiry. So susceptible is it to dampness that it is not a practical rope in sections where there is much rainfall or a constantly damp atmosphere.

Caring for Lariat

No two ropes are just alike. Each one seems to have an individuality of its own. When we get used to doing certain tricks with a certain rope, we find that no other rope seems to do them in just the same way. A roper cannot pick up another man's ropes and hope to do much with them. So when you get a spinning rope balanced so that it does a certain trick for you, take good care of it and do not leave it lying around. Do not let other people play around with your spinning ropes. Never use a spinning rope to lasso with. To do so may ruin the balance and destroy its usefulness for spinning.

Ropers become attached to their ropes. Often the oldest and least attractive is the dearest because the roper has it "educated" so that it does certain intricate tricks which other ropes will not do, which really means that it is properly balanced for those particular tricks. So "educate" your ropes, and then take care of them.

The mark of a roper is the way he coils his ropes when not in use. Whenever he is through with them, he coils each spinning rope up neatly in a little coil, not more than a foot across, and puts it carefully away, or hangs it up where it will not get damp. Loose care-less coiling is not done by good ropers, and no roper would ever leave a rope lying on the ground or floor.

Spinning Rope Dealers

Good spinning ropes and catch lariats are often diffi-cult to obtain. For the convenience of purchasers you will find a list and prices of all ropes recommended in this book inserted inside the back cover. They can be obtained through the people mentioned, or through any spinning rope manufacturer.

Made in the USA
Lexington, KY
10 December 2016